D0889667

I LOVE ANNUITIES . . .
AND YOU SHOULD TOO!

ALL THE BEST!

[signature]

ALL THE BEST

I LOVE ANNUITIES . . . AND YOU SHOULD TOO!

See How the Modern "Annua" Can Fit into Your Retirement Portfolio and Other Retirement Ideas

JAMES E. FOX, CEP, CSA

Library of Congress Control Number: 2015907296
ISBN: Hardcover   978-1-5035-6875-4
                 Softcover   978-1-5035-6876-1
                 eBook   978-1-5035-6877-8

Printed in the United States of America by BookMasters, Inc
Ashland OH
September 2015

Rev. date: 07/24/2015

To order additional copies of this book, contact:
Xlibris
1-888-795-4274
www.Xlibris.com
Orders@Xlibris.com
700958

CONTENTS

DEDICATION

To my wife, Sharon. As my business partner, you have seen our company grow in leaps and bounds over all these years. You have run our business like clockwork as I have followed and pursued my dreams. I could not have had nearly the success in this business if it weren't for you. I love you.

ACKNOWLEDGMENTS

First and foremost, I would like to thank our loyal clients, without whom we are nothing; my mom who always supported me to find my next dream; and my two beautiful sisters, Kathleen and Lynn, who have always supported me but also showed me courage through the loss of both my brothers-in-law in the last year. The pain you both have endured has given me tremendous strength. I would also like to thank my two dear friends, Jim Hoeflinger and Mike Topp. Jim, your faith in God when you lost your wife, Marie, to cancer truly showed me that faith conquers all. And, Mike, I can't show appreciation enough for your having the gumption to bring me into this business almost thirty years ago. You saw something in me that I didn't see in myself. Thanks also to Xlibris Publishing Company who have encouraged me to write this book and have supported me every step of the way. And a special thank-you to Jonathan Widran, my editor, who helped guide me through the process of writing this book.

INTRODUCTION

As a veteran of the financial services industry, I realize the importance of the position I have been placed in to help others. As our industry has evolved, we have taken on a greater responsibility to make sure we do right by others through adherence to ethics and acquiring as much education as we possibly can. After being in the business for over twenty-five years, I've come to really appreciate what we do and how we do it to the point where I am now mentoring others in our business. The key word that I stress to all in our mentor program is "lifetime" because it gives peace of mind to seniors who fear outliving their money. I love the television commercial with the college professor who is conducting a study for the Prudential Life Insurance Company, asking people who the oldest person is that they know. I also enjoy the ad that has people pulling a blue ribbon until their money runs out (usually before they expect). And the woman looks up and says "I better rethink this thing." Those commercials portray exactly what our clients fear most—running out of money.

Lifetime income annuities may not be a good fit for all, but for those who have them, they are wonderful supplements to their Social Security and pension payments. For these reasons, I have to be fully educated about the workings of the modern annuity. We have an obligation to make sure guaranteed lifetime annuities are part of our financial planning process because of the wonderful peace of mind these products provide. I like to call them "sleep assurance" because they ensure that you can sleep well at night, and so can I.

The financial services business has been rewarding to me and my family because we have the opportunity to change the lives of people who rely on us to stay current, educated, and licensed with trust, integrity, and service as the foundation that sets us apart from other businesses.

The next time I write a lifetime annuity product, I will be proud of what I have done for my client. As the baby boomer generation retires (over ten thousand people per day), people in this demographic need us now more than ever. We have the platform, and now is the time to use it. Coach Mike Ditka of the Chicago Bears once said, "The past is history, the future is a mystery, and today is a gift. That's why it's called the present." Let's take the gift of a lifetime income annuity and give it to my clients today so their future will no longer be a mystery. Guaranteed!

My goal for this book is to educate you on the workings of the modern annuity and other retirement ideas by keeping it simple and basic so you can fully understand and decide if these plans are a good fit for your retirement portfolio and strategies.

Please check out our Web site at www.foxfinancialgroup.net to learn more about our company, watch educational videos, read testimonials, and contact us.

CHAPTER ONE

HOW I BECAME KNOWN AS THE "SAFE MONEY GUY"

Instead of writing out my whole life story, I have decided to use excerpts from an interview and article called "Safe Money Guy" which was written in 2014 and was seen on many prominent business dot-com outlets, including Bloomberg Businessweek, MarketWatch, and Yahoo Finance!

The article opens with two headlines that capture the essence of what I and my firm Fox Financial Group, Ltd. are all about. The first says "Safe Money Guy" Jim Fox Has Focused Almost Exclusively on Lifetime Income Annuities for over Ten Years." The subhead reads, "The Twenty-Five-Year Financial Services Veteran's Chicagoland-Based Fox Financial Group Serves Hundreds of Clients with 'Integrity, Trust, and Service' as Their Number 1 Goal."

The text of the piece is as follows:

Jim Fox's wide range of talents, interests and passions have led him to play many unique roles throughout his life.

The Chicago native scored a basketball scholarship to Lewis University in Romeoville, Illinois, played hoops for years, has run multiple marathons, plays golf regularly and served for several decades as a high school and collegiate basketball official. As the "music guy," he plays guitar, mandolin and harmonica and has played in a traditional Irish band for years—including a performance before thousands of people at the Chicago Irish Festival in Grant Park. As a "charitable guy," he works with Children's Memorial Hospital, helping families who are struggling with terminally ill kids and other related issues.

But it's in the financial services world where Fox has scored his most impressive shots and played his most influential gigs. Hundreds of satisfied clients of his Burr Ridge (Southwest Suburbs) based firm Fox Financial Group, Ltd. know him as the "Safe Money Guy," dedicated in recent years to "Safe Money Management" via guaranteed lifetime income annuities, or more specifically, Fixed-Indexed Annuities with Lifetime Income Riders.

As a 16-year former registered representative of FINRA (Financial Industry Regulatory Authority), he witnessed and personally experienced the market crash in 2008, this became Fox's company calling. Beyond his home region in Northern Illinois, he has clients in Missouri, New Mexico, Florida, Michigan, Indiana, Wisconsin and Ohio.

In addition to being quoted in *Forbes* and *Advisor Today* in the March 2015 issues, Fox is also contributing co-author of world renowned professional development trainer Brian Tracy's book *UNcommon*. Throughout the many changes in the industry since he launched his firm in the early 90s—and his shift in focus from being a full service Medicare supplemental insurance, long term care and life insurance brokerage to retirement planning—he has been dedicated to three pronged goals of Integrity, Trust and Service.

"I have always believed that if you're not all three of those things, you will fail as a business," he says. "In a largely referral based industry, earning people's trust can only be achieved by doing business the right way."

Fox's extraordinary career has been marked by a strong entrepreneurial spirit, commitment to clients' evolving needs and his embracing of powerful new opportunities that came his way. While working his first post-college job as a truck driver for a delivery company, someone there suggested his personality would be great for sales. With his natural gifts as a "people person," who has been told more than a time or two that he's like an open book, he quickly rose through the ranks and became sales manager over seeing a small staff.

Not long after, a longtime friend and fellow hoops player who had become a General Manager of MetLife put in a good word and application for Fox at the large insurance company. The flexible schedule, unlimited income potential and the chance to help people proved irresistible. By his mid-20s, just three years after becoming an insurance agent, Fox was a branch manager making six figures, with dozens of agents working under him.

"The money was great but I wasn't happy," he recalls. "I found myself working 60 hours a week and feeling angry trying to motivate people who were basically resistant to that. In the insurance business, you're only as good as your next sale. People's schedules were flexible and they took full advantage of that, sometimes taking the summer off and trying to hit the goal figures they set for themselves around the holidays. MetLife still uses my phrase, 'It doesn't take a year to do a year's job.' My agents seemed to prefer to wait as long as possible to hit those numbers."

Believing he could be more effective dealing with people on a personal level than being a manager, and that it would be more rewarding working with clients on a one to one basis, Fox—along with his wife Sharon, who had worked for an attorney for years—launched Fox Financial Group, Ltd. 23 years ago. It was a mutual decision, predicated in part by their desire to have more flexibility to spend time with each other and their family. Though he had expertise in running a business, this involved an extraordinary leap of faith.

When he tells the story of building a successful family run business since then, he likes to use the phrase, "the proverbial rest is history." But the dynamics its evolution and expansion demand a more detailed telling, starting with Sharon's transition from simply serving as her husband's assistant to wearing multiple hats, including handling payroll, answering phones, ordering supplies and overseeing the operation as office manager. The "group" element involves working with accountants and attorneys who handle all the tax and legal work.

Though the name has remained the same, Fox Financial Group, Ltd. was a very different company in the beginning. Fox set it up as a full service insurance brokerage that also sold securities, mutual funds and variable products. In the early 2000s, he began adding more mutual funds and set up trusts, wills and variable universal life (VUL) insurance designed to help people avoid paying estate taxes as part of their estate planning.

When the market crashed in '08, everything changed. Fox himself lost thousands in investments, and Sharon reminded him, "If we lost that much, how do you think your clients are feeling?" Realizing that his current business model was not sustainable with the markets down and so unstable, he immediately canceled his security license and began focusing exclusively on guaranteed lifetime income annuities.

Fox had actually been selling annuities among his large array of services since 1996, but the crash, along with emerging new realities of the American economy made his decision a no brainer. The country has 77 million baby boomers and most of these people do not have pensions. Large companies either don't offer them anymore, or they were swallowed up in the crash. Instead they offer 401(k)s, and many retirees are forced to live off these and their monthly Social Security checks.

"Almost everybody lost something in 2008–09," he says, "and even if somewhere across the board your portfolio made a little money, it lost it somewhere else, whether from real estate depreciation, a 401(k), personal IRA or mutual fund. With everyone taking a hit, it was time to focus on guarantees and no risk, safe annuities."

Incredibly, or from another perspective, not surprisingly, when Fox changed the core principle of what the company became, business and clientele quickly doubled. For the past six years, his focal point has been telling new prospective clients—referrals and leads both—about exciting options for retirement planning. As before, these include estate planning, trusts and wills and long term care insurance to protect them later should they become incapacitated.

Even better, he worked with them on personalized strategies to create a stream of guaranteed lifetime income to help offset their pensions. He put clients into indexed annuities that cannot go down. He explains that in the worst case scenario, they might earn zero. "I love the phrase 'Zero is Hero'," Fox says. "Because if it made zero, that means if you had that same amount in the market you would have lost money. It's okay if it flattens. Another analogy I make is that it's like a staircase that can only go up. Each time you go up a rung, you cannot go backwards down the stairs because we lock in the rates every year on the anniversary of the day you took it out."

Fox couples that sense of safety and security with a lifetime guarantee of income, which happens in an unbelievable way for a husband and wife. When Fox puts together his plans, they decide how they want their income to stream in, so that if one of the spouses lives to be 105 years old, the survivor would still get the same monthly check. It comes every month regardless of age. Fox is sure to tell clients that he and Sharon personally have four of these plans, and he's not shy about showing them his statements.

"It's like a pension," he says. "We'll move their 401(k)s and IRAs they have been building and roll them over into something safe and guaranteed. Whether the market goes up or down, or whether you live to be 105, they cover both ends of the spectrum. I tell them that now when you go out to your mailbox to pick up your Social Security check, you get two checks."

Fox has been in the business long enough to know that many people come in needing education on the difference between variable and indexed annuities—and believes that any negative perception that annuities has is based on the variable ones, whose fortunes are tied to the volatility of the stock market and mutual funds. These are expensive, fee-ladened products that can lose principle if the funds go down. With indexed annuities, there is no risk, and with the education he provides comes peace of mind.

"The easiest way to sum it up is to tell them that their money goes into an indexed account tied to the S&P 500, or similar indices, i.e. NASDAQ and Dow Jones, so that regardless of market fluctuation, they cannot go down except for withdrawals," he says. "There are liquidity features which allow for withdrawals without penalties. There are only penalties for what we call 'early surrender,' so we advise clients not to cash their annuities in."

Many years after working with a behemoth like MetLife, Fox sees a great advantage to being an independent broker licensed with 50 different companies—a position which allows him to fit products based on a client's particular need rather than being captive to a large company's sales quota, and the company's certain plans.

"I have a wide array of different companies to work with as a gauge to the client's liquidity needs and beneficiary income needs. I have every potential client assist me, filling out a questionnaire, and from their responses I will create a particular plan based on those needs," he says. "More than ever these days, I am running into people who have problems based on their 401(k) and IRA, which have a required minimum distribution (RMD) age of 70 1/2. When these clients take their mandatory withdrawal, in some cases they don't want the money. They often want the money to go to their beneficiaries. The problem they have is wanting money to go to their kids but having to withdraw some of it. I work on plans that ensure that even when they take their RMD, there will still be money to be inherited by their heirs."

In the *Advisor Today* article, Fox is quoted relying on the words of one of his grateful clients. "This husband and wife were in one of our meetings holding hands as I told them how their guaranteed lifetime income plan would work and what their monthly income would be," he says. "The husband became all teary eyed and said, 'Jim, how can we ever repay you?' To me, right there, that's everything. That's why I do what I do. It's truly rewarding being able to help people, and it's an amazing opportunity that I could never have had being a manager at a big insurance firm. That man's gratitude is the reason I left and went out on my own."

....

As you can see, I love what I do. It's all about embracing the challenge of helping people achieve peace of mind. The following pages will give you a general breakdown of what we do and how we do it but also describe other retirement ideas and subjects, like life insurance, long-term care insurance, living trusts/wills, Social Security benefits, and reverse mortgages so you can enjoy a successful retirement. I hope this will be of benefit to you.

NOTES PAGE

NOTES PAGE

CHAPTER TWO
ANNUITIES 101

Over the years, many financial products have evolved into additional product offerings that may be more suitable for certain types of investors. Annuities are one such example. Annuities can offer many benefits for retirees and those who are approaching retirement. Although annuities can offer many positives for their holders, there are still some misconceptions with regard to how these products work and who they will benefit. Therefore, it is a good idea to have a more in-depth understanding about how these annuities work.

Annuities have been around for hundreds of years and were known as annua in the days of the Roman Empire. In AD 225, a judge in Rome named Ulpianus produced the first known mortality table. It was a lifetime stipend made once per year in exchange for a lump sum payment. Today's annuity has evolved exponentially to the point where some of the general public has no basic knowledge of how they work. This chapter is dedicated to educating you on the basics and to help you determine if they should be an integral part of your retirement plan.

Let's first take a look at the different kinds of annuities that exist today. The first one and the one that gets the most negative attention is the variable annuity. Most articles I have read do not promote them in a positive light because they have high fees i.e., mortality fees, expense fees, and front-end load charges (commissions). They also have high risk because of the fact that they are tied to mutual funds. Variable annuities have a large range of investment options. Most common are fund portfolios that give a rate of return typically on the performance of the options you choose. They are securities that are regulated by the SEC (Securities and Exchange Commission). The purchase payments and the periodic payments you eventually receive will vary because of the fluctuation of the mutual fund. In general, this bad rap has filtered into the common belief that all annuities are bad, which could not be further from the truth. I myself have helped dozens of clients into these variable plans, but my belief is that they are more appropriate for younger investors, not people who are already retired or about to retire.

Then there is the immediate annuity. This annuity is set up to pay you an income for a set number of years, usually five, ten, fifteen, and twenty years. You make your deposit, and the life insurance company—only life insurance companies can offer annuities—will pay a fixed rate for a set period. Once the allotted time of payments has passed, the income stops, and there are no remaining funds left. They typically will pay a higher monthly check because of the shorter duration compared to a lifetime payment.

Next is the fixed annuity. You have the straight fixed kind that pays a flat interest rate for a set period, similar to a CD, i.e., 1.0 percent for five years, or invest in a fixed annuity paying 2.5 percent. (Most fixed annuities usually pay a higher fixed rate than a CD.) Or you can invest in a fixed-indexed annuity, also nicknamed the hybrid annuity. This is because it offers similar features as the immediate, variable, and fixed annuity without the risk and high fees. The indexed is the one "I LOVE" and is also the one I have most of my own personal money invested in. I will explain this in more detail later. Most annuities grow on a tax deferred basis, which can really affect your growth compared to a CD, which requires a 1099 tax form be sent annually, unless the monies are in an individual retirement account. No 1099 will be issued in that case.

The other way of explaining tax deferred growth is the beauty of compound growth. Compounding means the money you pay in taxes each year stays in the account, which will calculate at triple compounding. Confused? Let me explain. If you have $100,000 in a CD at 3 percent, it would earn $3,000 minus the taxes. If you were in the 28 percent tax bracket, you would net 2.16 percent or $2,160 for one year for a total net value of $102,160. That same $100,000 tax deferred at 3 percent would gross you $3,000 or $103,000 after the first year. In year 2, you start out with $102,160 in the taxable CD versus $103,000 in the tax-deferred annuity.

Now stop and think of the beauty of this over ten years! You get interest on your principal, interest on your interest, and interest on the taxes you would have paid each year, i.e., "triple compounding." And nowadays, most CDs are at 1 percent if you're lucky and fixed annuities are at 3 percent. Imagine how the numbers work now. Of course, you have to pay the taxes later, but there is a heck of a lot more money to pay them with. It equates out to 4.17 percent gross on a 3 percent deferred plan. To really check on these numbers, go to interestcalculator.org.

Another advantage of annuities is the option to name a beneficiary or a trust to take over the account after you die. They avoid probate, which could save you thousands of dollars in court costs, legal fees, and months of time. They are backed by the insurance company that promotes them, followed by that state's guarantee association as much as $500,000 per individual—depending on the state you live in. Most plans do not charge an early withdrawal penalty for death (a huge misconception by the general public). Annuities are very popular in the state lottery system. If the winners elect an annual payout instead of lump sum, guess who pays you? A life insurance company's annuity! Usually, it's a twenty-year immediate annuity.

A topic that has come to light recently is discussed in a press release dated October 24, 2014, by the United States Treasury Department in conjunction with the IRS (Internal Revenue Service). It stated, "Most Americans should start putting at least 50% of their retirement and pension money into annuities to guarantee a pension." Wow, are you kidding me?

I've been saying that for years, and now two of our largest money management government agencies are saying "buy annuities"? An advisor to the World Bank, Dr. Jeffery Brown, a world-renowned economist, says, "Annuities are one of the most important investments we have." He knows a thing or two about creating income. He was only one of seven individuals appointed by the president of the United States to the Social Security Advisory Board and has been an advisor to China to help evaluate their Social Security dilemma. One more publication I have used for years is the *Barron's* magazine report titled "Special Report—Best Annuities— Retirement: With Their Steady Income Payments, Annuities are Very Hot." Wow, again! One of the world's most popular investment magazine companies for risk investors has annuities featured on its cover? Who knows? Maybe I'm a visionary!

Did you know that Ben Bernanke, the former chairman of the Federal Reserve Board, owns annuities? Or that one of the most famous money men and motivational speakers in the world, Tony Robbins, has annuities? Or that Steve Forbes has a plan he calls "longevity insurance"? The list goes on and on. I think you're starting to get the picture. Just this past January, *Insurance News Net Magazine* quoted a LIMRA study that found that one third of households in the United States with assets of $500,000–$999,000 own at least one annuity. It also found that 38 percent of households with assets of $100,000–$500,000 have at least one annuity. In 2014 alone, more than *$50 billion* were invested in annuities, and that's not even counting variable annuities.

The list goes on and on. On June 6, 2005, Mr. Ira Carnahan from *Forbes* magazine wrote in an article titled "Do-It-Yourself Retirement: A Better Bet If You're Worried about Running Out of Savings Might Be to Invest Some of It in an Immediate Annuity." Also from *Forbes*, on May 25, 2009, Mr. Scott Woolley wrote, "Economists who study the retirement market have long been sold on the merits of annuities and frustrated by consumers aversion to them." On August 8, 2007, Mr. Jeff Opdyke from the *Wall Street Journal* wrote, "Income annuities can assure retirees of an income stream for life at a cost of as much as 40% less than a traditional stock bond and cash mix." Also from the *Wall Street Journal* dated March 8, 2011, Ms. Lavonne Kuykendall wrote, "Many investors approaching retirement think they have no need for annuities, but the lifetime income guarantees offered by these insurance companies' products can add security to portfolios that are mostly composed of stocks and bonds."

By what you have just read, you can see that annuities are more popular than ever, and you now have to consider them as part of your retirement plan.

NOTES PAGE

NOTES PAGE

CHAPTER THREE

THIS IS *NOT* YOUR GRANDFATHER'S ANNUITY

Assembling the optimal retirement plan is critical for today's seniors given that their retirement years will likely be much longer than that of their parents'. Most troubling is the fact that many of today's retirees do not have the comfortable pension plans to offset the ever-increasing risk of living a long life when money is invested in risk. This can now be viewed as double risk. Many individuals focus on traditional investments and investing styles in the hopes of capitalizing on the same returns on those investments that our parents had. For others, though, finding the perfect plan may come in a new form, such as in the use of fixed-indexed annuities. After learning what they are, it may be clear that this is the right step to take for your own retirement plan, depending on your current exposure to market risks and running out of money.

Fixed-indexed annuities are a type of annuity that gives yields based on the return of an index, most often the Standard &

Poor's (S&P) Fortune 500. They are similar to other annuities in that the conditions and terms of the annuity depend on the plan terms and payout options. The unique benefit that sets indexed annuities apart from other annuities is the fact that they offer their owners the ability to grow their accounts as their index increases while being fully protected from any downturn in the index. Further, they contain a unique feature called annual reset, which locks in your increases in the account value at the end of each year while locking in this new higher amount. I will be talking more about this later.

Indexed annuities have been around for twenty years; the first was a plan from Keyport Life on February 15, 1995, called the Key Index Plan, a product that seemed too good to be true, an annuity that guaranteed a floor (no losses) and could also give clients the upside potential of the S&P 500 gains.

Before thinking that this offering is too good to be true, you must understand that insurance companies have to place caps, spreads, and participation rates on your annual account increases during the up years to protect their solvency, given that they are fully shouldering the risk of the down markets. That's how they can answer the questions of how they can do this. This is too good to be true! I will also be discussing later in this chapter the caps and spreads and how they work. Further, you should note that these products are not designed to offer high returns like mutual funds and stocks, but they are designed so you will *not* have the risks like mutual funds and stocks, and historically they have paid a higher yield than CDs and the like.

Most annuities do have surrender penalties for early withdrawal. A common ten-year plan would have penalties that reflect 10 percent penalty in year 1 and downward to 1 percent penalty in year 10. But they also give you several liquidity options. For example, you can withdraw 10 percent annually before and after your annual anniversary. For example, if your annuity anniversary date is June 1, you can take 10 percent on May 31 and 10 percent on June 2 for a total of 20 percent if needed at that time. You can also take withdrawals for required minimum distribution (RMD) at age seventy and a half or sooner, nursing home stay (called well-being options), annuitization, income, and death benefit proceeds—all with no penalties. So people who dismiss annuities and say you can never get your money out have not done their homework, or they don't want you to put your monies in them because they want to put them in other investment vehicles.

Fixed annuities are good for those who do not want to bet their retirement lifestyle on potential "returns." They are better suited for those looking for a way to protect their hard-earned retirement savings while having the potential to grow at a modest rate. Education is key, so be sure to seek out a retirement income planner to see what your best options are.

Macroeconomics is a term used quite often in the investment world because it has to do with "overtime." The phrase is one that I live by every day. One of the great fears that most retirees have (including myself) is the thought of outliving their money. With technologies and medicine, people are living much longer; in fact, studies have shown that someone alive today will live to age 120. Today's average life expectancy for a married couple is that at least one spouse will have a 25 percent chance to reach age ninety-seven. If this is not a wake-up call for people to start preparing for their retirement, I don't know what is. So what can we do about it?

One of the great features of most modern annuities is the income rider. This rider gives the investor a guaranteed (yes, I said it, guaranteed) income check for life. They can also be designed for spousal continuation as well. (Remember, 25 percent will live to age ninety-seven?) Regardless of what age you live to, there will be a guaranteed income check similar to your Social Security checks. But the big difference between the guarantee income rider and Social Security is when the second person dies, whatever money is left in the annuity account will go to a named beneficiary, usually within three weeks, whereas the Social Security pension checks stop. In fact, Social Security will want a partial refund for the remaining month that was paid after the date of death, unless you died on the first day of the month.

The annuity with the lifetime guarantee income rider we more often than not put our clients into is the indexed annuity. The deposit they make can be in a single premium or flexible premium depending on the companies and the plans that they offer. This type of annuity is geared toward partial market returns without the risk. Let me explain. A fixed-indexed annuity, also known as a hybrid annuity on several Web sites and publications, is a tax-deferred funded vehicle between you and a life insurance company that earns interest that is tied to equity-based indices. Most common is the Standard & Poor's Fortune 500 (the top five hundred United States publicly traded stock companies). In some cases, they can also be linked to the NASDAQ, Dow Jones Industrials, and other indices. The indexed annuity is tracked on the market indexed. It can be followed on a daily basis but more of on a monthly and annual term, usually paid on the annual anniversary date. The indexed annuity is virtually identical to a fixed annuity, except for the way the interest is credited. For example, a $100,000 indexed annuity can earn between 0 percent (that's the floor, or minimum) and whatever the maximum might be, i.e., cap rates. Whereas a fixed annuity might pay 3 percent for a set period and earn $3,000 per year in this example.

The insurance company invests your premium with tens of thousands of other premiums and usually will purchase bonds and a one-year S&P 500 call option. (We will discuss this more in the next chapter.) This is the way the company is linking the equity index to your premium. The company will take the risk and offer you a 0 percent return or floor if the market loses money, which if you think about it, means you cannot lose on a downward spiral like we saw in 2000, 2001, 2008, and 2009. The tradeoff is what is known as the cap rate, participation rate, and spread rate.

The cap rate that I alluded to in the previous paragraphs refers to the max you can earn on a monthly or yearly basis. If the plan offers a 1.5 percent monthly cap, it would equate to the most you can earn in one year, which is 18 percent or 1.5 percent times twelve months. They look at your monthly returns on each of your monthly anniversaries and take a snapshot of what the return was. Then they average it over the period of one year.

If there are more down months or one really bad month or months, it will affect your overall monthly average on the annual return. The annual cap works similarly, but the index return is based on a one-year return snapshot on your one year anniversary. Let's say, for example, that the S&P 500 is trading at 1,900 points and the one year market return raises the S&P to 2,100 points. That would reflect a return of roughly 9.5 percent. If the annual cap is 4 percent, you would earn 4 percent. If the market return is 3 percent, you earn 3 percent. (The most you can earn is 4 percent, and the least is your floor at 0 percent.)

One of the nice features is called an annual reset. It means that each year, you start over at whatever the indices are trading at, which means if the market goes down, you will reset at the lower amount on your one-year anniversary. For example, if your opening account date was 6/1/15 and the S&P 500 was trading at 1,950 points, and on 6/1/16, it was trading at 1,875 points, you will reset for the next year at 1,875 points, which will give you movement to go up in the following year. It is important to understand that this is not a security, and you are not actually investing in the market. The insurance companies are using the S&P 500 or similar indices as a crediting method on which to average your annual return.

Next is the participation rate. This formula is based on capturing market returns based on a percentage of your participation. For example, if you have $100,000 in an 80 percent participation rate plan and the one-year return is 10 percent or $10,000 on a $100,000 deposit, you would earn $8,000 or 80 percent.

A spread rate works on the premise of the company earning the first portion of the return, and you earn the rest with no cap, i.e., if $100,000 in a 2.5 percent spread and the market returned 10 percent, you would minus out the 2.5 percent spread (company keeps). You then would earn 7.5 percent or $7.500 in this example. Most of the spread plans offer no caps, which I favor because after the 2.5 percent in my example, there is no limit on the earnings once the 2.5 percent is reached.

Now conversely, if the account only earns 4 percent, your earnings would be 1.5 percent (4 percent minus 2.5 percent spread equals 1.5 percent net). Keep in mind that these plans are not designed to lose any principal. If the market is down –7 percent, you would earn zero, which is not such a bad thing. I like to use the phrase "Zero is hero." Think about this: you have the upside of the market with caps, spreads, and participations but without the down trends of market losses with the zero floor and potential for gains with no losses. Wow, pretty nice, isn't it?

Please look at the following page to see the graph on capturing the gains with no losses in the market as we have just previously discussed. The graph represents just one of my favorite companies called American Equity's Historical Return called Real Benefits. The graph is based on actual credited rates for the period shown. This plan is no longer available, but it gives you an idea of how you can capture the upside of the market and have a zero floor (Zero is hero!) in a down market. Powerful stuff.

American Equity Investment Life Insurance Company, West Des Moines, Iowa, has only approved this advertisement (form 15-AE-0350). American Equity has not reviewed or approved any other content that may appear in this book. American Equity is not responsible for the same. American Equity does not make any representations about any product or services discussed in this book beyond those in this specific advertisement. When appropriate, American Equity urges you to contact a qualified tax, legal, or investment professional to discuss your specific needs. This form is copyrighted by American Equity.

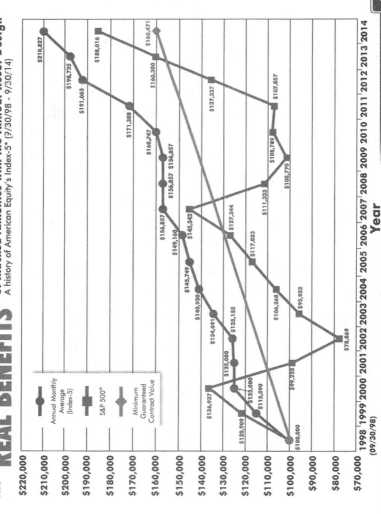

Let's refer to this as your "A Bucket" or your cash. As you see in the chart, your "A Bucket" is increasing the first years and then flattens out in year 2, or the years 2000–2002. But if you notice, that same year you opened the account if those same monies were invested in an S&P 500 account, after year 4, or 2002, your $100,000 deposit would have been worth $78,869. The annuity in this example is worth $125,155. There is no downturn in the annuity because it has a floor of a zero return if the market is negative.

If you look down the chart to the year 2009, you will see the annuity has flatlined again, or paid zero. But the S&P 500 account would have been worth $100,770. So after eleven years in this example, you would have broken even, and the no-loss annuity would be worth $156,857.

This is what I call having your cake and eating it too! Now the tradeoff in this chart shows that on the positive growth years, the gain in the S&P 500 outperforms the annuity because of the cap rate tied to this particular annuity. My thought is, so what? I can have some of the growth of the S&P 500 without any of the losses. Can you imagine looking at this chart and you retired in 2009? Since no one knows what's going to happen in the market, this type of process has to give you peace of mind. Heck, even the minimum guarantee value outperformed the S&P 500 from 2001 through 2005 and again from 2007 through 2012. Now you should have a better understanding of how the cash grows in your "A Bucket."

NOTES PAGE

NOTES PAGE

CHAPTER FOUR

GUARANTEED LIFETIME INCOME

In the previous chapter, we discussed how the modern annuity has evolved into a wonderful retirement funding option. Now I would like to discuss the awesome retirement-guaranteed income rider. Most companies offer these types of riders, but they may vary greatly depending on the amount of monies invested, age, liquidity needs, marital status, deferment time, and fees.

Most indexed annuities lifetime income benefit riders have fees ranging from 0 percent to 1.5 percent on average. These fees determine the growth potential and the income payouts. Each company is different, so make sure you work with a trusted and experienced retirement planner. I'm amazed at how many people I talk to who do not have a plan for retirement. Most wealth management advisors help people accumulate assets but don't know how or want to know how to distribute it. That's because they get paid on the amount of money under management which I will go into further details in chapter six.

What we will now discuss is wealth distribution, not wealth accumulation as in the previous chapter. Retirees are filled with dreams of what they anticipate their retirement will be like—seeing and doing things they only dreamt about. But without a reliable income stream, those dreams could be a shattered reality rather quickly if the market turns sour. I like to use the phrase "double dipping." Can you imagine if you retired in the year 2000 or 2008 and started taking withdrawals at the same time the market did a prolong crash? You would have partially liquidated your nest egg twice, once for income and once for market losses. These plans are designed to never have this happen again. In Tony Robbins's new book called *Money: Master the Game* (great read, by the way), he also quotes Dr. Jeffrey Brown by saying, "Income is outcome." Tony also refers to guaranteed lifetime income as "income insurance. A guaranteed way to know for certain that you will have a paycheck for life without having to work for it in the future—to be absolutely certain that you will never run out of money!"

I myself love all the new terms that describe guaranteed lifetime income. I have already told you I love the term *sleep assurance*, but there's also *Sleep Insurance*™ by American Equity, "longevity insurance," "income insurance," "income is outcome," and many others. These quotes give you a general description of how wonderful peace of mind can be, i.e., sleep, insurance, longevity, assurance. Sounds pretty good, doesn't it?

Now let's go into the workings of these income plans. As you have now deposited your hard-earned money from your investments like 401(k)s, IRAs or similar accounts, the insurance companies invest your money, as discussed in the previous chapter, into the S&P 500 or other indices. Remember that was your "A Bucket", or your cash account. The income you generate will depend on several factors as we previously discussed, i.e., age, marital status. The calculation for the income on the next page will show you how the income will vary depending on the previously mentioned questions. In this income calculation, I like to call it your "B Bucket." Remember, the "A Bucket" is your growth and cash, and now the "B Bucket" is your income and pension.

Please refer to the income calculator on the next page.

Years Deferred	Age	LIBR Calculator Details Income Account Value	Guaranteed Annual Payment
1	65	$117,700.00	$5,943.85
2	66	$125,939.00	$6,485.86
3	67	$134,754.73	$7,074.62
4	68	$144,187.56	$7,714.03
5	69	$154,280.69	$8,408.30
6	70	$165,080.34	$9,244.50
7	71	$176,635.96	$10,156.57
8	72	$189,000.48	$11,151.03
9	73	$202,230.51	$12,234.95
10	74	$216,386.65	$13,415.97
11			
12			
13			
14			
15			
16			
17			
18			
19			
20			

*Maximum issue age varies by product and state. Age of youngest insured is used for joint Contracts

This example assumes no withdrawals. This is not a complete description of all rider provisions, nor is it intended to predict future performance. Please refer to the brochure and contract for details. Producers, please contact the Marketing Department for current rider availability.

Lifetime Income Benefit Rider:
1. By choosing the 7.0% Income Account Value (IAV) Rate you will be charged a 0.90% annual fee from your contract value. Interest grows until the earlier of payments beginning or the end of the IAV period. If payments not elected by 5th contract anniversary, growth of IAV will stop unless client elects to reset accumulation period. The fees may change if the IAV period is reset but will never be more than the maximum rider fee. IAV only used to calculate lifetime income payments. It is not part of the underlying Contract or available for partial withdrawal or in a lump sum.
2. Benefit provided by Lifetime Income Benefit Rider (ICC14 R-LIBR).

American Equity Investment Life Insurance Company, West Des Moines, Iowa, has only approved this example (form 15-AE-0351). American Equity has not reviewed or approved any other content that may appear in this book. American Equity is not responsible for the same. American Equity does not make any representations about any product or services discussed in this book beyond those in this specific example. When appropriate, American Equity urges you to contact a qualified tax, legal, or investment professional to discuss your specific needs. This form is copyrighted by American Equity.

In this income calculation, I will use a sixty-four-year-old male, single with $100,000 from a 401(k) rollover waiting seven years to take his first guaranteed income withdrawal which will also cover his required minimum distribution schedule.

The Internal Revenue Service requires anyone with an individual retirement account (IRA) to take distribution from their account at age seventy and a half or at the latest by April 1 of the year after they turned seventy and a half. If you do not take your distribution in this time frame, the IRS will levy a 50 percent penalty for the total amount not withdrawn.

I'm using the American Equity Life Insurance Lifetime Income Benefit Rider Calculator, known as the Bonus Gold Plan, for your reference which by the way is one of my personal favorites. In this calculation, you will notice growth on the income account value each year that he did not take the income stream, also known as the rollup period. The guaranteed income growth is at 7 percent each year for seven years. At the end of the seventh year, his guaranteed income would be $10,156.57 for as long as he lives based on his single (unmarried) status. If he died in two months or in twenty years, whatever amount of money left in his "A Bucket" would go to his heirs/beneficiaries. You do have a 0.90 percent annual fee that comes out of your cash account, or your "A Bucket." Once you start your income, the 7 percent rollup growth will stop at this time.

Some plans offer options to take the income after just thirty days which works out well for someone who just retired and needed income immediately. There are some insurance companies that don't even charge a fee for this income rider, but usually to offset this, the annual rollup will be less. For example, American Equity Life Insurance Company has a 0 percent fee plan that has a 4 percent guaranteed rollup for ten years compared to the 7 percent rollup at 0.90 percent fee. Nowadays, 4 percent is nothing to sneeze at with no fees.

It's important to remember that all annuities have the age fifty-nine and a half rule. You can invest in these annuities before age fifty-nine and a half, but if you take a distribution or withdrawal before that age, you will pay a 10 percent IRS penalty, regardless of if it is an IRA or not, qualified or nonqualified. In some cases, you can take a hardship withdrawal for health, education, and welfare, but this has to be approved in advance.

As you are now taking your guaranteed lifetime income, you need to be aware of how the taxes are levied. This is an important part of your monthly budget so you can calculate net income instead of gross income. Almost all annuities are tax deferred, meaning they are taxed at time of withdrawal in a variety of ways. Fortunately, they grow at a compound rate which means higher growth, but eventually Uncle Sam wants his turn.

Simply, if your annuity is an IRA, then 100 percent of the amount withdrawn is taxable as ordinary income subject to your own specific tax rate. If it's not an IRA, then the gain is taxable under "the last in, last out" guideline. For example, $100,000 of a nonqualified or non-IRA plan at 5 percent growth in year 1 would be worth $105,000. So let's say you decided to take a withdrawal of $10,000 out of your plan. You would only be taxed on the $5,000 gain. The original $100,000 was already taxed. It gets a little more complex if you have an immediate annuity or if you annuitized an older annuity plan. The nonqualified annuity payments are part principal and part taxes spread out over the term of the payment, e.g., with a ten- or twenty-year payout, your annual 1099 tax form will be spread out over the ten or twenty years. The 1099 will give you the breakdown that can be explained by your CPA. You should always consult your accountant for all your tax questions, since everyone's situation is different.

Another great feature that the guaranteed lifetime income plans offer through your "A Bucket" or your "B Bucket" is the premium and/or income bonuses that most companies give you. They can be received in one of two ways. The first is a cash bonus, or premium bonus, which is given on top of your premium/deposit. For example, a $100,000 deposit with a 10 percent cash bonus would net you $110,000 upon issue of the plan. Pretty nice. "Free money." The second way to receive a bonus is on your income account or "B Bucket" which gives you a bonus on your guaranteed income. For example, if you open your new account with $100,000 with a 20 percent bonus on your income plan, it would now open at $120,000 to start your income pool. Pretty amazing when you see how the income calculator shows how the income will be paid out.

So to recap, you have an indexed growth account with no losses in the market ("A Bucket") with a minimum guarantee and a growth-filled roll-up income account ("B Bucket") that pays you and/or your spouse a guaranteed income for life regardless of market fluctuations. I hope this will give you a better understanding of how your growth ("A Bucket") and your income ("B Bucket") work. Remember, income is outcome.

One more great feature that companies are now creating as these income riders evolve is the use of crediting methodologies. A handful of plans available now offer an annual compound increase of income if the markets go up, even over and above your guarantees. I like to look at it like an inflation protector. You get your guaranteed roll-up each year you don't take your income, and they will add the market returns on top of that based on a daily fluctuation over each year. The numbers can be staggering on a positive S&P 500 growth each year or years.

As long as you adhere to the withdrawal limits, lifetime income payments are guaranteed for life. Even after you start your income, your maximum lifetime income benefit rider payment will be reset based on your new highest point of the account value and then multiplied by the payout percentage that was in effect when you started the income. Pretty cool stuff. Guaranteed income plus potential increases?

I spoke earlier about how they can do this. What's the catch? Well, to explain as simply as possible, when you purchase a fixed-indexed annuity, the majority of your monies are invested in a balanced and diversified bond portfolio. The bond will produce a return based on interest rates. It's very safe and has little or no market risk. It traditionally will give the same rate regardless of market fluctuation.

The second part of the investment goes into the purchase of a call option. Simply put, a call option is a vehicle where a company can profit from the market because of its increases. The option is not invested directly in the commodity or stock but will make a return on the profits of the market movement. Most of these call options are in one year S&P 500 movements. The insurance companies will credit the interest growth on these options to the consumer's gains that will traditionally have a cap, spread, or participation rate as previously explained in chapter three.

A little confusing, but with some of the most talented actuaries and mathematicians in the world developing and monitoring these plans, you can capture market gains without directly being invested in them and also have a guaranteed lifetime income benefit rider.

NOTES PAGE

NOTES PAGE

CHAPTER FIVE

RISK VERSUS SAFETY AND SUITABILITY

In *Webster's New World Dictionary*, the definition of risk is stated simply "the chance of injury, damage, or loss." Such simple words, yet they're powerful in their meaning. In the eHow.com definition, they state, "As an investor, the risk is inherent with more involvement needed than just knowing your investment could go up or down." It means if you are not actively involved in your investment, you have now left it up to chance. Of course, you have hired a professional to help you in this risk endeavor, but you really have no control. I love the line "You're in it for the long haul." Just after you called your broker to complain because your monthly statement was thousands less than it was the previous month In Wikipedia. org, the term they use for avoiding risk is *risk aversion*. It is used as a concept in economics and finance based on the behavior of humans while exposed to uncertainty to attempt to reduce that uncertainty.

"Risk aversion is the reluctance of a person to accept a bargain with an uncertain payoff rather than another bargain with a more certain but possibly lower expected payoff." For example, a risk-averse investor might choose to put his or her money into a bank account with a low but guaranteed interest rate rather than into a stock that might have high expected returns, but this also involves a chance of losing value. We all have been averse to market loss at one point or another during our lifetime, but once you approach retirement or are already in retirement, risk aversion is more prevalent.

The decisions you make now regarding risk can stay with you for a lifetime. There are three basic investment options we have today: banks, insurance companies, and Wall Street. Each offers a wide array of investment vehicles. Banks traditionally have been the safest but offer the least in returns, i.e., CDs (2 percent if lucky), money market and savings accounts (0.50 percent if lucky), and checking (0.10 percent). Some banks are now even offering annuities through life insurance companies, which I find very interesting—and I wonder why this is! Hmm . . .

We have already discussed the features of annuities that insurance companies offer. So let's delve deeper into Wall Street type investments. When investing in various types of Wall Street investments (as I like to call them), you have a very wide array of options. Most common are stocks and mutual funds. A stock investment consists of buying a particular company's stock, i.e., General Motors or IBM, where you are purchasing an investment in one company. On the other hand, a mutual fund is invested with hundreds of other investors buying shares of hundreds of companies' stock. It still has risk, but the risk is spread through multiple companies' return instead of just one, which in many cases should lower the risk. But this is not always the case.

In the stock arena, you can choose from common stocks, preferred stocks, penny stocks, dividend stocks, and shorting stocks. These are usually purchased through a stockbroker who will manage it at a fee. In the mutual fund arena, your options are endless. There are hundreds of companies/brokers you can go through to invest, i.e., Fidelity, Edward Jones, and Smith Barney. These companies typically will invest in the Dow Jones, NASDAQ, S&P 500, and International Funds. They too will charge an annual management fee and/or load charge to manage the account.

You have several other investments that offer risk and reward like commodities, options, and hedge funds, to name a few. These investments come with very high risk. But also have the potential to give very high returns. I hope this gives you the principles of the three basic options you have.

When considering risk, there are so many variables to consider, like: age, risk tolerance, time frame, amount to be invested, liquidity needs, retirement date, goals for your beneficiary/inheritance, other investments you may already own, your financial needs, net worth, income, tax status, investment experience, financial objectives, and intended use.

Like any investments, there has to be a layer of suitability, meaning not all plans are good for all people. As professional advisors, we have to make sure that the investments we recommend are a good fit for your goals. It has to be "suited" for your particular needs.

The National Association of Insurance and Financial Advisors (NAIFA), Financial Industry Regulatory Authority (FINRA), and the Securities and Exchange Commission (SEC) have all established guidelines for money managers to follow when assisting the public on their investment options. A number of states have specifically addressed suitability for over a decade, starting when the National Association of Insurance Commissioners (NAIC) first introduced he suitability transaction model regulation no. 275. It had also been a common practice for state insurance regulators to address suitability concerns through their respective states' Unfair Trade Practices Act. More recently, states have adopted the revised version of the model regulation, as updated in April 2010 (the NAIC Model Regulation). (Visit www. NAFA.com for a complete list of states that have adopted the updated 2010 model.) And well, before the 2010 version of the model regulation, carriers had voluntarily developed and implemented suitability standards on their own.

FINRA's suitability rule (FINRA Rule 2111) is based on a fundamental FINRA requirement that brokerage firms and their associated persons (sometimes referred to as brokers, financial advisors, or financial consultants) deal fairly with their customers.

FINRA's suitability rule states that firms and their associated persons "must have a reasonable basis to believe" that a transaction or investment strategy involving securities that they recommend is suitable for the customer. This reasonable belief must be based on the information obtained through the reasonable diligence of the firm or associated person to ascertain the customer's investment profile. The rule requires firms and associated persons to seek and obtain information about the customer, as we discussed four paragraphs earlier.

To help insure that customers receive suitable investment advice, firms and their associated persons are required to learn as much about a customer's investment profile as possible before recommending a securities transaction or investment strategy. FINRA's Know Your Customer Rule (FINRA Rule 2090) may also cause firms to ask questions to open and service your account.

The Securities and Exchange Commission (SEC) requires firms to attempt to obtain a customer's name, tax identification number, address, telephone number, date of birth, employment status, annual income, net worth (excluding primary residence), and investment objectives regarding certain accounts. Firms also are required to put procedures in place to verify the identity of any person seeking to open an account. Before opening an account, a firm must obtain at a minimum the name, date of birth, address, and identification number (for example, a Social Security Number) of a customer.

These guidelines are all put into place to assure that not only are these recommendations suitable for you but to also protect the advisor for errors and omissions that might have been overlooked.

Not all investments are suitable when it comes down to risk or safety. Safety not suitable? Sounds strange but true! All advisors must adhere to the suitability guidelines and stay educated and current through continuing education to make absolutely sure that our recommendations are suitable.

In an article that featured our company in *Insurance News Net Magazine,* I was asked several questions. One question was how my career has evolved to the point that we changed our company business model to focus on annuities. "Why the switch?" Well, after selling securities, i.e., mutual funds and variable plans, I explain that the suitability issue has become more prevalent than ever. As I have gotten older, most of our clients have gotten older as well, and I felt that putting an investor's retirement plan into annuities was more suitable for that age demographic based on their income needs now. Suitability versus Risk has to be part of every conversation.

NOTES PAGE

NOTES PAGE

CHAPTER SIX

WHY DON'T THEY LIKE US?

In this chapter, I would like to focus on a very important topic that I feel needs to be addressed: the "them versus us" mentality. There are many investment options to choose from in the world today. Not all are right for everyone, and not all are wrong for everyone, just as some advisors are better fits for certain individuals than others. That's what makes our industry so wonderful—options! In over a quarter of a century in this business, I have now seen more separation between risk managers and safety managers than I have ever seen before. For some reason, this division has taken on a life of its own, with advisors saying things like, "Don't do this or that because of this or that." Meaning, don't invest with that guy or girl because that product is bad because of this. I get it. We are all competing for the public's business, and it's our business, our passion, and our livelihood.

More recently, I have noticed that the "them versus us" posturing has risen to a whole other level. I was very fortunate to be asked to give a quote in *Forbes* magazine (3/2/15) regarding our company's predictions for the New Year and beyond. It was very flattering to be asked, and I said that the baby boomer generation needs to start building retirement accounts with guaranteed lifetime income riders now more than ever because most company pensions are going by the wayside.

I decided to subscribe to *Forbes* magazine. As I was reading the first issue of my subscription, I noticed at the very end of the magazine—it was the last page, as a matter of fact—an advertisement from a company on the West Coast that struck a nerve with me. Here I was, all excited to be quoted in "the" *Forbes* magazine. As you can imagine, I was thrilled to no end, and I was just about to finish when there it was: "I HATE Annuities, and you should too!" in big bold letters. My heart sank. I felt anger and betrayal. Did Steve Forbes do this to me himself? Once I calmed down and I realized that it wasn't Steve himself who was responsible, that it was just an advertisement, my heart stopped beating like the percussion section at a Notre Dame football game.

Now after finally calming down but still frustrated, it occurred to me that I had told my clients, family, and friends, "Hey, I'm in March's *Forbes* magazine"—and they might see this ad. It was upsetting because most of our clients, family, and friends have annuities. How am I going to explain this? Why should I have to explain this? Luckily, I saw that the issue that my quote was in did not have the advertisement, so I was not put in scramble mode.

Still bothered by this ad, I decided to do some research and look into what makes this company tick. After interviews, teleconferences, receiving their company brochures and material, I came to rather an insightful conclusion that I will delve into later. In my findings, though, I saw that the company's founder has an extensive background in stock investing and has built a company of brokers which promotes and sells his strategies all over the country. Whether I liked him or not, the company's advertising is everywhere, i.e., magazines, Internet, and now even a television infomercial. I guess the fact that he has this stock empire of brokers everywhere has enabled him to afford such an advertising campaign and that money is no object.

In many ways, this marketing blitz was a wake-up call to all of us in the investment world. Money breeds money, and I thought, maybe we should start to spend our money talking about our wonderful products and, I suppose, defending ourselves through the promotion of these products as well.

So now after weeks of research and pondering what to do next, I decided to dedicate a chapter in this book that I was already writing. In many ways, after reading that advertisement, my philosophy has kind of reversed in fortune. Not only has he shaken the foundation of what we do, but now he has helped us in the advertising of it! Thank you! My attitude has changed 180 degrees. I now talk about his company in every home and business I go into because he struck a chord of discussion of "them versus us" attitudes that needed to be addressed. Another big "thank you" is that it inspired the title for this book, *I Love Annuities and You Should Too!* It was written in part to try to explain to potential clients that annuities with a guaranteed lifetime income rider could be a good fit in their retirement goals and also to now defend ourselves from the advertisers hating them.

Not all brokers, I realize, hate annuities, and this is not a full-blown war; but many of our clients have told me that this broker or that broker said that annuities are no good, and you shouldn't have one. Well, the time has come to start defending ourselves from these types of money managers. I would never make a blanket statement that no one should ever buy or hate stocks. They just have to be a good fit.

I'm not going to just discuss the company out West but all brokers who promote the hatred toward annuities in advertisements and in speech. Through my research, I learned that the 'I Hate Annuities' company itself is what I would like to address and some of the bullet points it mentions. This should give you an idea of how they try to get your attention through fear of the topics you might not be sure of or forgot to ask. Again, thank you for now making this subject part of my everyday routine. One of the most glaring bullet points is "Watch Out for the High Commissions You May Be Paying." Like all professionals, you are going to pay for services rendered in some way. Some variable annuities charge an upfront load charge (commissions), usually around 4 percent. I personally do not have these plans in my investment strategies for our clients any longer because of the risk they have. Our company's average commission is 5 percent depending on the plan and company chosen. The great feature of this is, you don't pay the commission to me; the company pays it, which means 100 percent of your money goes to work for you. So if that is one of his bullet points—and many other brokers work the same way—let's look at how they are compensated.

Many brokerage accounts are now managed on a fee-based structure with the average commission/management fee being 1.25 percent annually. So let's compare. I put a client into an annuity. For the sake of argument, it is $250,000 for a twenty-year duration. At 5 percent, my commission would be $12,500 as a one-time payment. If you put that same $250,000 into a managed brokerage account, with an annual fee of 1.25 percent for that same twenty-year period, and let's say the account earned 0 percent for that period, the total fee/ slash commission would be $62,500! Now if that brokerage account grew in value at all, you would pay the 1.25 percent on the growth as well. Hmm . . . $12,500 versus $62,500? Now who is making the "high commissions"? It's these kinds of scare tactics that have caused so many discussions in the "them versus us" mentality.

Next is the claim "They Charge Several Layers of Fees." This is true on variable annuities but not on fixed, indexed, and immediate annuities. These ads blanket all annuities, so you have to read the fine print and ask lots of questions. If you really want to see a breakdown of your mutual fund and/or 401(k) account fees and you're not using a fee based planner, you can research all these funds on this Web site: www. personalfund.com. You will be shocked at all the fees and charges that are hidden in these types of plans. Most of these plans average over 3 percent annually.

Next is "The Serious Downsides of Fixed-Indexed and Variable Annuities." What this alludes to is the fact that you cannot capture the highest growth from on the returns because of the caps, spreads, and participation rates that were previously discussed in chapter three. Sure, there are caps, participation rates, and spreads. This is how the companies can keep your money safe. It limits the potential for all of the returns—but remember, the floor is 0 percent. If the market crashes, you earn zero. Remember, "Zero is hero." Can they say that? Obviously not!

Next is "Careful! If You Need Your Money Early, You May Have to Pay a High-Surrender Fee." Heck, why not throw another scare tactic at the public? You're on a roll. Anyone who owns or promotes annuities should know that they have early withdrawal penalties. That's how they can give safety, guarantees, growth potential, and floors. But they also can give liquidity features, as also discussed in chapter three, i.e., 10 percent annual withdrawals, etc. But they do not discuss that in their advertisements. I think you are starting to get the picture.

There is one more bullet point that I would like to address in the ad: "Want Out of Your Annuity? We May Rebate Some or All of Your Annuity Surrender Penalties." Sure, but at what cost? If you read the fine print, you can go into their Web site and read the terms and conditions. Let me save you the trouble. It reads, "If you determine your annuity may not be the best option for your financial goals, we may compensate you for some or all of your annuity surrender fees incurred when liquidating your annuity."*

Sounds great, doesn't it? Sounds pretty straightforward, yes? Let's read the asterisk next to it: (1) Limited Time Offer: The offer is available for a limited time only. We reserve the right to cancel, suspend, or modify the offer at any time and for any reason without notice. (2) The offer is valid only to qualified investors. (3a) "Conditions: The maximum surrender costs will depend on the actual surrender cost of the annuity. (3b) Any surrender costs that we agree to pay will be payable in equal quarterly installments over several years (which means you have to keep your money with them to get all your surrender fees paid). (4) There is no guarantee that any annuity proceeds will achieve any specified level of performance or that performance will be any higher than what could be achieved with an annuity. Really?

I have had several clients who have asked me about this program. I took a long hard look at what this offer is. They will pay the surrender charges over time, but it is paid with a "reduction in fees" on a quarterly basis. In other words, as they manage your portfolio, they charge you fees. They will charge you less if you surrender the annuity and move it to them. Their fees for management are high to begin with, so a reduction in fees merely brings them back to the rest of the money management world.

Also, if you look at the fine print, you'll see that you must stay with the company to receive the reduction in fees. If you leave, their obligation to pay for your surrender charges is lost. So let me get this straight. If you leave the investment company, you lose your right to get back the surrender charges? Funny! To me, that sounds like a surrender penalty for leaving early. Ironic, isn't it?

Wow, they are not kidding—read the fine print and asterisks. I know I'm beating this thing up, but you have to understand—these selling tactics do grab your attention, but at what cost?

At the bottom of the ad, they mention risks: "There is no guarantee that any proceeds from any products mentioned above (managed by the investment firm) will achieve any specified level of performance, or that performance will be any higher than what could be achieved within that product. Investing in securities involves risk of loss. Past performance is no guarantee of future returns." Sounds pretty comforting, yes? So if you lose money, is that not a penalty as well?

The subject I would like to address now is the discussion and advertisements that most money managers use regarding investment returns. Most money managers like to use the term *average returns*. The problem is that the market does not give you the average returns. It gives you the actual returns that work out to be average. Confused? For example, if a person invests $100,000 into a managed account and the return is −50 percent in year one, the account would be worth $50,000 at the end of year one. Pretty simple math. Now let's say the account grew +50 percent in year two! How much would that account be worth? Most would say −50 percent plus 50 percent equals 0 percent averaged return. Not so bad, right?

Now think about this for a second. Let's look at the actual return: $100,000 − 50 percent = $50,000 after year 1. Year 2 is +50 percent. So you have to calculate it at $50,000 + 50 percent = $75,000 actually. So the −50 percent +50 percent does not equal zero. It equals − 25 percent actually. So many investment firms will advertise at the end of two years the average return is 0 percent, but the account's actual return lost 25 percent. How can this be, you ask? Very simply, the "actual" return can never be the "average" return at any time you have a factor of a negative number. I recently saw a Web site called Money Chimp that really explains this in detail, and you can see for yourself the differences. The Web site is www.moneychimp.com/features/market_cagr.htm on which you can enter any range of years and see the average versus the actual returns. Very powerful stuff.

If I seem a little hell-bent on educating our clients and future clients on the understanding of the markets, it is because there is a lot of bad information out there touting one investment over another. Our company's focus is on guaranteed lifetime income. It might not be right for you, but for someone to say *all* annuities are bad and "I hate them" leaves one to ponder their motive.

When was the last time your broker asked you "How can we set up a retirement plan for you?" They usually don't because they are paid on assets under management for a fee. Do you really think that they want you to take your money out? No matter what anyone tells you, or sells you, there isn't a single portfolio manager, broker, or financial advisor who can control the primary factor that will determine if you will outlive your money. They can't, for the simple reason that they cannot predict future growth or losses. But we can!

Well, they might "hate" annuities, but I now know why! (Thanks again!)

NOTES PAGE

NOTES PAGE

CHAPTER SEVEN

WHAT YOU DON'T KNOW ABOUT SOCIAL SECURITY CAN COST YOU!

Social Security! Wow, has this become a hot topic? Every time you open a newspaper or your mail, someone is running a seminar on the subject. It's the new way for investment guys to market their products, and rightfully so. These seminars are packed with baby boomers who are about to retire and want to know what options they have. The general feeling is to take it at age sixty-tow or just wait until their full retirement age. There is so much more, and the public is finally learning that maybe they should consider different options instead of only choosing only age sixty-two or sixty-six.

Pres. Franklin D. Roosevelt created the Social Security program in 1935. It was set up to alleviate poverty for the elderly during the Great Depression. At the time, the average life expectancy was only age sixty-two, and you couldn't get your first check until age sixty-five. Very few were receiving this new government program. The other aspect of the program was there were forty people contributing, and only one was collecting. One of the most glaring stats now is only three are contributing for every one person that is collecting, and the life expectancy for a male age sixty-two is now age eighty-one and that of a sixty-two-year-old female is eighty-five. The odd of one married couple's spouse living to age ninety-five is 24 percent. I'm not a math major, but as you can see, the numbers don't add up.

The program is actually pretty new. It's only covered two generations of pensioners—our grandparents and our parents. That's pretty new considering how old the first humans were. As recently as the eighties, most retirees had pensions, over 60 sixty in fact. Now you're very lucky to get one. Now most companies, if they offer anything, have a 401(k), and then you have to put your own money into it to get any of theirs. And it comes with fees that eat away at your growth. Most companies only contribute 3 percent on average, which is much less than the old traditional pensions. Because of these statistics, most pre-retirees are looking much deeper into all their options for securing a successful retirement. One of these options is Social Security. If you had asked someone what is their biggest asset, they would probably say their home or their 401(k). Well, most of the time they would be wrong—it's their Social Security check. The average single collector earns almost $1,300 per month, and a married couple earns on average almost $2,200 per month. Over a lifetime, this is most people's largest asset but also their largest income. It makes sense to learn as much as possible about it, hence the Social Security seminar movement.

Over your lifetime, if you worked for an employer that collected payroll taxes, you would contribute 6.2 percent into Social Security every check. If you were self-employed, it would be 12.4 percent. You have paid into it, and now is the time to collect it. Managing your Social Security benefit should be part of your entire retirement income process. Social Security is the starting point of your retirement income analysis. Not everyone understands how Social Security benefits work or how to maximize the value of these benefits. When you add a spouse to the picture, your planning can become quite complex. So let's delve into the basics and your options.

Your year of birth is the main starting point. You have to determine when you can collect full benefits, and this is done through your year of birth. See the chart on the next page.

DETERMINING YOUR FULL RETIREMENT AGE

YEAR OF BIRTH	FULL RETIREMENT AGE
1937 or earlier	65
1939	65 and 4 months
1940	65 and 6 months
1941	65 and 8 months
1942	65 and 10 months
1943–1954	66
1955	66 and 2 months
1956	66 and 4 months
1957	66 and 6 months
1958	66 and 8 months
1959	66 and 10 months
1960 or later	67

Social Security Administration

Normal Retirement Age, 2015.

To maximize your benefit, you must consider your start date so you can get the largest amount of lifetime payments. The problem is many Americans cannot wait until full retirement age to maximize this option. But mistiming your start date could cost you hundreds of thousands of dollars. As long as you have paid into the program for forty quarters, or ten years, during your lifetime, you will qualify for benefits. The numbers are based on "credits." You're fully insured if you have all forty credits. At age sixty-two is when Social Security Administration will determine what your starting benefit will be. That's why over the years, they have always said what your average check will be, not an exact number. They factor in all monies received up till age sixty-two, and only then you get the exact amount. At that point, they take your highest thirty-five years of earnings and average them out. If you worked less than thirty-five years, the missing years will average and calculate at zero dollars.

Now that you understand the basics, let's go into your options. If you're age sixty-two, you can now collect benefits but at a cost. See the second chart on the following page.

DETERMINING YOUR BENEFIT REDUCTION FOR EARLY RETIREMENT (AGE 62)

YEAR OF BIRTH	BENEFIT REDUCTION
1937 or earlier	20%
1938	20.83%
1939	21.67%
1940	22.50%
1941	23.33%
1942	24.17%
1943–1954	25%
1955	25.83%
1956	26.67%
1957	27.50%
1958	28.33%
1959	29.17%
1960 or later	30%

Social Security Administration

Benefit Reduction for Early Retirement, 2015

As you can see, based on the year of birth, the benefit reduction can be as high as 30 percent. I know some people do not have the luxury of waiting, but by just delaying it for a couple of years, it could mean thousands over a lifetime.

Okay, so let's now look into delaying the payment. For each year you delay the start, you get delayed retirement credits. Your benefit amount will increase by 8 percent per year up to age seventy! Wow, this is huge over a lifetime. Now remember, if you delay to age seventy, that's where it ends, and you receive no more retirement credits. An example would be someone who would have received $2,000 per month at age sixty-two, minus the benefit reduction, would earn $1,500 per month, or $18,000 per year, which equals 75 percent of your full retirement benefit age of sixty-six. If he or she had waited until age sixty-six, they would get the full benefit at $2000 per month, or $24,000 per year. If they waited until age seventy, they would receive $2,640 per month or $31,680 per year.

Another option is the file and suspend. It's a way to maximize benefits for married couples. You apply for benefits at *full* retirement age and immediately suspend your income for a later date. Now the lower earning spouse applies for spousal benefits of the higher earning spouse. He or she will get one half of the higher-earning spouse's benefit. Pretty neat. It really works well if the higher-earning spouse is still working up to age seventy. He will collect higher benefits because of the delay, and the lower earner will also get the higher amount as a survivor benefit if that person should predecease.

Obviously, as you can see, I could write an entire book on this subject alone. Some of the other options could be just as important. You have the back payment option. This is when you are older than your full retirement age and you file for benefits backdating to your full retirement date and get a lump sum check going back to that age. You can only apply for this when you are six months or longer past your full retirement age.

Another option is the restricted application. This is designed similarly to the delay option, where he or she would collect his or her spouse's benefit and delay theirs until age seventy and then collect their own full benefit to the maximum amount. Only one spouse can do this option at a time.

One of the most confusing options is the survivor and divorce option. The surviving spouse of a deceased worker can collect benefits even if they never paid into it. They can start collecting at age sixty at the earliest, unless you are disabled. Then the age is fifty or later. The only catch is that they have to be currently married for at least nine months prior to death. If both were receiving benefits at the time of death, the surviving spouse will only get one check of the higher amount. FYI, if you remarry before age sixty, you lose the spousal benefit.

The divorce option can benefit multiple people. Many don't know if you have married multiple times for a minimum of ten years each, all the divorcees would receive a benefit as long as they didn't remarry. The famous comedian and television show host Johnny Carson had multiple ex-wives receiving benefits. FYI, you need to be divorced for at least two years before you can receive benefits.

Let's glance at some of the ages and numbers on the chart on the next page. You will get a clearer picture of the ages that will impact your decisions.

Because the Social Security process involves several important decisions and a careful consideration of alternatives, we urge you to work with your financial professional to be sure you make choices that are appropriate for you.

At age fifty: If you are the widow or widower of a person who worked long enough under Social Security, you can begin receiving benefit as early as age fifty if you are disabled, and the disability started before or within seven years of the worker's death.

At age sixty: If you are a surviving widow or widower, you can begin survivor benefits but at a reduced rate.

At age sixty-two: If you are a qualifying individual, you can now begin to receive Social Security benefits but at a reduced rate. By waiting longer, though, you could receive a larger monthly benefit.

At age sixty-five: You are eligible for Medicare on the first day of the month you turn sixty-five. You might want to consider enrolling because if you do not enroll prior to or during the month you turn sixty-five and wish to enroll later, you may be required to pay a higher premium for Medicare Part B.

At age sixty-six: If you were born between 1943 and 1954, you are now at full retirement age and eligible for full Social Security benefits. By waiting longer, though, you could receive a larger monthly benefit because of delayed retirement credits. Spousal benefits, however, do not continue to grow after your full retirement age.

Between age sixty-two and two months and age sixty-six and ten months: If you were born between 1955 and 1959, your full retirement age is age sixty-six plus two months for each birth year after 1954, as seen in the previous pages.

At age sixty-seven: If you were born in 1960 or later, you are now at full retirement age and eligible for full Social Security benefits. By waiting longer, though, you could receive a larger monthly benefit because of delayed retirement credits. Spousal benefits, however, do not continue to grow after full retirement age.

At age seventy: If you have not started receiving Social Security benefits by this time, you should know that waiting longer will not increase your benefit.

Here are some additional numbers that could impact your decisions:

- If you take your benefit at age sixty-two, you will earn 75 percent less compared to age seventy.

- Sixty million Americans are currently receiving benefits.

- Fifty-two percent of couples and 74 percent of unmarried people have this benefit.

- $15,720 is your maximum earnings if collecting benefits before age sixty-six. If you have more income than that, they keep 50 percent of your benefits.

- $41,880 maximum earnings if collecting benefits age sixty-six or older. They keep $1 for every $3.

- $2,642 is the monthly maximum you can earn during your lifetime, which would represent thirty-five years contributions at $117,000 per year in earnings.

- Thirty-five percent of the work force has no money saved for retirement.

- 7.5 percent wait to take Social Security after their full retirement age.

Obviously there are many options to choose from, including disability benefits. Even going to seminars cannot cover all the options in the time allotted. It's best to seek out a qualified retirement planner who can answer your questions.

For additional information regarding your specific needs, go to the government's Web site at www.ssa.gov or another very informative site, www.socialsecuritychoices.com.

In April 2011, Social Security statements were no longer automatically mailed to workers unless you were age sixty or older. In September of 2014, they resumed mailing paper statements every fifth year of your age, i.e., forty, forty-five, fifty, etc. If you want to see a statement now, go to another Web site: www.ssa.gov/mystatement.com. Or you're always welcome to visit your local Social Security office.

I hope this has given you some ideas on your situation, and I hope these Web sites assist you in a successful retirement.

NOTES PAGE

NOTES PAGE

CHAPTER EIGHT

IS A REVERSE MORTGAGE
RIGHT FOR ME?

Of all the retirement options available to most seniors, the one that gets the most questions regarding their misunderstandings is a reverse mortgage. Many people are very confused of their workings and the problems they perceive as a "bad idea" usually from someone that they have asked who has no clue on how they actually work. Now let the record show they are not for everyone, and I'm not suggesting you should run out and get one today! But for the right situation, they can be a good fit for part of your retirement strategy. This chapter will identify some of the misconceptions out there and also educate on the facts.

Larry McAnarney, in Oakbrook, Illinois, is my resource and go-to guy on the subject. He has helped hundreds with these programs for over sixteen years. He and I have spent many hours discussing the pros and cons, and I have come to the conclusion that many people should consider one.

History of Reverse Mortgages

The history of reverse mortgages dates back to 1961 and has evolved dramatically over the last fifty-four years. A young loan officer, from a local savings and loan company in Portland, Maine, made a loan to a widow of his high school football coach so that she could stay in her home after her husband's sudden death and the loss of his income. I don't know the exact details of the transaction, but the idea of using housing wealth as a source of income without a mandatory monthly payment was born, today known as a reverse mortgage.

In the 1970s, several private banks began to offer various versions of reverse mortgage type loans. These loans were not reverse mortgages, but the common theme with all these programs is that it gave seniors access to money from their home equity without monthly payments; however, these early private loans were not protected nor insured by the federal government as they are today. In 1987, Congress passed a reverse mortgage pilot program called the Home Equity Conversion Mortgage (HECM) demonstration that included a program that allowed the Federal Housing Administration (FHA) to insure reverse mortgage loans. President Reagan signed the act into law on February 5, 1988, authorizing FHA to insure reverse mortgage loans; and in 1989, the first FHA-insured reverse mortgage was recorded in Fairway, Kansas.

Since 1989, reverse mortgages have continued to develop and grow in popularity, allowing older Americans to access a portion of their home equity through a Home Equity Conversion Mortgage (HECM), which is the official name for the FHA-insured reverse mortgage program. The program continues today, allowing seniors to access a portion of their home equity while never making a mandatory monthly payment.

The Reverse Mortgage Stabilization Act of 2013 was signed into law by President Obama on August 9, 2013, which authorizes the Secretary of Housing and Urban Development (HUD) to establish and enact additional policy requirements to improve the fiscal safety and soundness of the home equity conversion mortgage insurance program. Prior to the implementation of this act, major changes to the HECM program had to go through Congress which was very political and very slow. Now by notice or mortgagee letter, any requirements determined necessary to improve the fiscal soundness of the program can be made by HUD without congressional approval.

Because of the reauthorization act and changes HUD has already made to the HECM program, financial advisors, mainstream media, and the retirement planning community in general has endorsed the HECM line of credit program as a viable and important retirement planning tool. Many financial firms have already started looking at housing wealth via the HECM program as the tax-free fourth leg in retirement income distribution planning. The Financial Industry Regulatory Authority (FINRA) which regulates the financial planning industry issued a policy alert on April 30, 2014, changing its position on the use of housing wealth in retirement.

"FINRA is issuing this alert to urge homeowners thinking about a reverse mortgage to make informed decisions and carefully weigh all of their options before proceeding. And if you do decide a reverse mortgage is right for you, be sure to make prudent use of your loan." (Source: FINRA Investor Alert April 30, 2014) You could replace the term *reverse mortgage* with any financial product such as annuities or securities, and the alert would be just as relevant.

Reverse Mortgage Basic Requirements

- Borrower must be sixty-two years or older, if married, at least one spouse must be sixty-two or older.

- Must be legal owner(s) of the home at application.

- Must be the primary residence (no second homes or investment properties).

- One to four family, HUD approved condos, and manufactured homes (land home) are eligible properties.

- Maximum loan amount is calculated based on the age of the youngest borrower, interest rate, and home value.

- Lender requires first lien position.

- No monthly payments are required; voluntary payments are permitted.

- Fixed and adjustable rate/line of credit programs.

- No defined term (loan becomes due on the youngest borrower's 150th birthdate).

- Property must meet FHA appraisal requirements.

- Federally insured loan.

Common Reverse Mortgage Misconceptions

If I do a reverse mortgage, will the bank own my home?

The answer is the homeowner retains full ownership of their home throughout the life of the reverse mortgage. Just as with any conventional home mortgage, the lender places a lien on the property to ensure the bank is covered for any money that is borrowed. Many people, including many bank officers, attorneys, CPAs, and even financial advisors, think that for some reason the bank or government takes ownership of the home and that the borrower has basically sold their home to them. This is simply not the case and remains the biggest myth about reverse mortgages.

This misconception probably started because of some early private "reverse mortgage type" programs in which the bank shared the property appreciation with the homeowner. This was known as equity share, and there are still companies that are trying to offer this type of mortgage today. However, there are no FHA-insured reverse mortgage programs that include any type of equity sharing.

Can I have a mortgage on my home and still qualify for a reverse mortgage?

Yes, you can have a mortgage and qualify for a reverse mortgage; however, the proceeds available in the reverse mortgage must first be used to pay off liens on the owner-occupied property.

Are reverse mortgages only for people who are desperate?

In recent years, the use of housing wealth through reverse mortgage has become an excellent financial planning tool to complement and enhance retirement income planning. As you will learn in this chapter, there are several powerful strategies of using housing wealth in a comprehensive financial plan.

Retirement Strategies Using a Reverse Mortgage

Annuitizing housing wealth and converting it to tax-free guaranteed lifetime income is a very powerful strategy and will greatly increase the survival rate of a financial plan. Adding monthly income to any retirement plan will increase the probability of success that the retiree will not run out of money in their lifetime. Of course, the biggest concern for retirees is running out of money in their lifetime, and I would add to that, paying the high cost of medical care. The strategies outlined below show various ways the reverse mortgage can complement and supplement a comprehensive financial plan. The HECM line of credit is very versatile and flexible, as changes in the distribution of proceeds can be changed and adjusted at any time, unlike many other financial products.

Strategy 1: Standby line of credit/deferred monthly income

Many top financial advisors refer to the reverse mortgage standby line of credit as the emergency reserves or deferred guaranteed monthly income strategy. The idea behind this strategy, as with most of the strategies using a reverse mortgage in a retirement portfolio, is the balance of funds available in the HECM line of credit as a growth rate which will compound in the borrower's favor. A hypothetical example: a homeowner has $200,000 available in a HECM line of credit. The $200,000 available balance will grow at a rate equal to the index, usually the one-month or one-year London Interbank Offered Rates (LIBOR) rate, plus the margin. For the sake of this example, let's assume the rate is fixed at 5.0 percent. If the growth rate remained at 5.0 percent for one year, the available funds in twelve months would be $210,232; and in twenty years, the available funds would be $542,528. This is because of the tenth wonder of the world which is compounding that I discussed in chapter two.

In this example, you are using compounding in your favor to defer use of funds until needed. At any time, funds can be accessed as needed by the homeowner or converted to lifetime monthly income or both. The longer the HECM line of credit is allowed to grow and compound, the greater availability of future funds and greater guaranteed monthly income. Reverse dollar cost averaging and sequence of return risk can be significantly mitigated with the use of an HECM line of credit.

Another amazing aspect of the HECM line of credit is that no matter what happens to the economy or housing market, the growth in the line of credit will continue and cannot be cancelled, frozen, or reduced. Since the line of credit growth rate is tied to the index, in this case the LIBOR index and not the housing market, it is truly a hedge for both a declining housing market as well as a hedge for inflation. Many financial advisors are well aware of what happened to their clients' traditional standby line of credit when our

Great Recession hit. At a time when their older clients needed ready cash, the banks froze, canceled, or reduced their lines of credit. In contrast, clients who had a HECM line of credit in place were shielded from this liquidity shock because the lender is obligated to lend remaining funds in the HECM line of credit.

Strategy 2: Deferral of taking Social Security (as discussed in chapter seven)

This is similar to the deferred monthly income strategy, except its purpose is to provide monthly income to the homeowner so that Social Security income can be deferred until age seventy. Assuming income is needed during the deferral period, using the reverse mortgage to provide monthly proceeds can provide income needed for living expenses while allowing for a greater lifetime Social Security benefit through deferral. Once Social Security benefits begin, you can choose to stop the monthly payments from the HECM and begin taking the increased Social Security benefit, or continue with both monthly income sources—your choice.

Strategy 3: Pay off a current mortgage with a reverse mortgage

There are two possible strategies with this option: (1) the HECM loan pays off a current conventional mortgage and frees up this monthly mortgage obligation, thus increasing the monthly household income because the homeowner never has to make a monthly payment to the HECM loan, so long as one eligible borrower remains in the home as their primary residence; and (2) refinance the conventional mortgage with a reverse mortgage, but continue to make a mortgage payment to the reverse mortgage. Making payments to a reverse mortgage is essentially the same as putting money into your HECM line of credit, which will then continue to grow and compound as described earlier. At any time this can be converted to monthly income or drawn in a lump sum.

Remember, no monthly payments are required in a reverse mortgage, so any payments are optional. But by making payments to the reverse mortgage, two things are being accomplished simultaneously: paying down the mortgage and increasing the growing line of credit for future retirement distribution options. Ask you banker about that and see if they understand what you are talking about. They won't.

Strategy 4: Reverse mortgage purchase strategy

Most people, including most realtors and builders, either aren't aware or don't understand that a reverse mortgage can be used to purchase a new home. Normally, as homeowners get older and their children start their own lives, the house may be too big, yard work, maintenance, and upkeep becomes too much, so they choose to sell the house and purchase a smaller home that requires less maintenance. Usually this involves using the cash from the departure home and paying cash for the new home. In a HECM for purchase program, approximately 50 percent of the purchase price of the new home can be financed with proceeds from the HECM for purchase program. This allows for more money from the sale of the departure home to be used for retirement income. For some seniors, they choose to increase the purchasing power of the new home by 50 percent. Believe it or not, many seniors who understand the power of this program choose to have more buying power and upsize in value and amenities rather than downsize.

What happens at the end of the HECM?

The second most common question: What happens when I die, or how long does the family have to satisfy the loan balance? Upon death or permanent departure of the last surviving spouse, the HECM loan becomes due. This means that as long as one eligible borrower or eligible nonborrowing spouse remains in the home, the loan is still in effect and is not due.

Once the home is unoccupied by a participating HECM borrower, the "due and payable" process begins and is very simple as long as the heirs or estate communicate their intentions with the lender. The clock starts ticking the day the last surviving spouse no longer occupies the house as the primary residence. The estate/heirs have six months to pay off the loan with up to two three-month extensions for a total of one year. These extensions are not automatic and must be applied for through the lender. The payoff balance is the amount borrowed plus accrued interest and government mortgage insurance, less any optional payments that may have been made.

HECM loans are nonrecourse loans, meaning that the borrower, their heirs, or their estate *cannot* be held personally responsible for any shortfall. If the loan balance exceeds the value of the home, the difference is paid to the lender from the FHA insurance fund. The lender is prohibited by HUD from seeking a deficiency judgment and looking for other borrower assets to make up the shortage. In a conventional mortgage, the lender will usually enter into a short sale agreement and then seek the remaining funds through a deficiency judgment to try and mitigate the loss through other borrower assets.

I hope this chapter has given you a basic understanding of the FHA-insured HECM program and a few basic HECM strategies that can be used in a comprehensive financial plan. As with any financial product, changes can and will occur to the HECM program; however, changes cannot be made retroactively to those who already have a HECM loan in place. Contact a reverse mortgage consultant for specific examples based on current program guidelines. For a detailed illustration, the consultant will need the age of the youngest borrower, estimate of property value, and the balance of any mortgages currently on the property. Before making any changes to your financial plan, contact me or your financial advisor.

"The bottom line to all these strategies, though, is pretty straightforward: reverse mortgages may work far better when they're done not as a last resort, but as part of an ongoing retirement plan." —*Michael Kitces, partner and director of Research Pinnacle Advisory Group*

"The new view of a FHA HECM reverse mortgage for wealth management firms is that the 'Highest and Best' use of HECM reverse mortgages is to improve a client's retirement plan—not rescue it. It is a view I've come to share after diving into FHA HECMs and their applications. There are a variety of ways to use them strategically to good advantage and hopefully very rarely as a client's last resort. My perspective comes from working with wealth management clients going into retirement with investment portfolios in the $500,000 to $4,000,000 range. Many of these clients could benefit from FHA HECMS." —*Thomas C.B. Davison, MA, PhD, CFP*

NOTES PAGE

NOTES PAGE

CHAPTER NINE

NOW WHAT SHOULD I DO?

In this chapter, I would like to focus on how all this information you have just read affects you —and what should you do about it. Or better yet, THIS IS YOUR CALL TO ACTION! The only way—research has shown—to have a healthy and successful retirement is to plan, get prepared, and do your homework. It's not just life insurance, long-term care insurance, living trusts, Social Security, reverse mortgages and annuities, but a combination of all these programs and strategies to assure your success.

In my first bestselling book I coauthored with Brian Tracy called *UNcommon* by Celebrity Press Publishing, I wrote a chapter about lifetime income benefit riders and their effect on the common man and how life changing they can be. I gave an example of one family in particular that these plans had a profound effect on that will stay with me for the rest of my life and hopefully theirs as well. (I touched on this in chapter one of this book, but I thought it should be reiterated.)

I had just finished explaining how their income will now increase exponentially and that they have reached the "magic number" that they had envisioned in their minds of income to retire comfortably. The couple held hands, and the husband began to get teary eyed. He asked, "Jim, how can we ever repay you?" By him saying those words so softly and gently, I too began to well up and thanked him, not only for being my client but for reaffirming that I am so blessed and fortunate to have a career where I truly can change people's lives, through all our "sleep assurance" programs.

I know I'm not all things to all people, but when considering a retirement advisor, I always ask potential clients to question all advisors in their research (because I know I'm in competition and everyone should get multiple opinions) and be sure to ask the following key questions: How many years have they been in business? Have they had any complaints? Have they been published? Written a book? Are they members of local Chambers of Commerce and Industry? Members of the Better Business Bureau? Been featured in magazines and on Web dot-coms? How much assets do they have under managements? Have you seen their testimonials? What companies do they work with? How many guaranteed income retirement plans have they set up (not how many clients do they have)? These questions will give you a clearer picture of their experience.

You can talk to five different planners and get five different answers on retirement planning, but there are truly only two questions that need to be answered. Do you want to spend it or give it? Many plans can address these two simple questions, but first you have to eliminate the risk of losing your money to offset the monthly income you have. Risk factors include market risk, nursing home, and death. One common denominator that no one talks about is longevity risk. *If you live too long,* this will have a direct effect on the risk factors I just described. You have to protect longevity risk as much or if not more than anything else. You have to ensure that your income will be permanent regardless of how long you live.

I like to use the rule of one hundred. What this means is subtract your age from one hundred. That is the percentage number you should have in risk. This is because as you take income from your portfolio, it's the timing of the returns, not the actual returns. Let's say your actual return over twenty years is 8 percent. Well, that's pretty good, you say. (Remember, that is your accumulation years.) Now let's say you started taking 5 percent per year. Chances are you will run out of money if the market drops at all, or at that same time, because actual returns are thrown out the window once you start taking withdrawals (remember, distribution years).

If you had retired in the nineties, chances are you did okay with your retirement account because there were no huge swings in the marketplace. But if you retired in the 2000s, it's likely that you took a huge hit. We all heard the stories of people having to go back to work because their 401(k) rollover became a 201(k), i.e., were cut in half. Very sad but true.

Let's look at some very basic numbers to show how market volatility can affect your income. Let's say you earned 7 percent on $100,000 year one. Simple math says it would be worth $107,000. And let's say it made another 7 percent in year two. It would now be worth $114,900. Now let's say in year 3 it went down –7 percent. It would now be worth $106,475. Now during that same period, let's look at a three year return of 2.25 percent. It would be worth $106,903. So to compare the two different funding strategies, as you can see, all it took was one bad year to take out two positives. 2.25 percent can outperform 7 percent in this example.

With five downturns in the market in the last fourteen years, who knows when the best time is to retire? I know I don't, and I'll bet nobody else does either. All it takes is one bad year during the distribution phase to change your actual returns.

In a recent article written by James Hopkins, Esq. (*Insurance News Net Magazine,* February 2015) titled "Americans Are Overconfident and Unprepared for Retirement," he brings out some glaring statistics on how unprepared we are as a society really are. He is the associate director of the American College New York Life Center for Retirement Income.

Hopkins wrote, "Today, Americans are underfunded for retirement anywhere from $5 trillion to $14 trillion. While this huge retirement savings shortfall is concerning, new research—the 2014 Retirement Income Certified Professional (RICP) Retirement Income Literacy Survey—from the New York Life Center for Retirement Income highlights an even more troubling point: Americans Know Very Little about Retirement Planning. The RICP survey quizzed more than 1,000 Americans between the ages of 60 and 75, with moderate to high levels of investable assets ($100,000 plus), on a variety of crucial retirement planning questions. The survey included both knowledgeable and attitudinal questions on a variety of important retirement planning topics, including Social Security, life expectancy, taxes, inflation, annuities, retirement income generation, medical insurance and long term care. Only 20% of Americans passed the test."

To me, this is very troubling because the demographic of this age group is mainly retirees and those who are about to retire. The survey shows to me that most are ill informed and have spent little time planning or overconfident regarding their own retirement. We as a population need to spend more time thinking about the key elements of retirement and retirement income. We as a nation have to spend more time on education. It's essential to start yesterday. You have heard the phrase before that most people spend more time planning their yearly vacations than planning their retirement. That's because it's boring and not fun. But this mentality has to stop. The time is now. In most cases, people know they need a plan but don't know how to go about it or who to trust. You don't need to have $5 million in your investments to start a plan.

I previously talked about a CALL TO ACTION. Tom Hegna, the motivational speaker and educator on retirement planning whom I have met in Las Vegas at a couple of business conventions, also promotes a call to action. I have read all his books, my favorite being *Paychecks and Playchecks* (another great read if you're retired or going to be retired). He likes to use the phrase "happy retirement steps."

Now picture this: I was in a hotel in Atlanta, Georgia, on another business trip, getting ready putting on my suit for this dinner engagement when I glanced over at the television, and there was Tom! I proceeded to turn up the volume, and he was talking about how to be "happy in retirement." I sat on the end of the bed tying my tie, listening to someone touting the very things I've been saying for years, things to prepare for when you're approaching retirement.

His steps are very similar to mine. He asks things like: Did you know if the primary breadwinner waits till age seventy to take Social Security payments (if you can wait), that your Social Security payment will go up a whopping 35 percent compared to if you had taken it at age sixty-two as I described in chapter seven. Like me, he also insists that people have to have long-term care protection through a rider on an annuity plan, life insurance plan, or private insurance so they won't be wiped out of all their savings. There are many of us touting the process of all these things to have a successful retirement.

To touch on this subject briefly, long-term care insurance is an essential tool you should have, based on statistics that we have recently seen. The odds that one of a married couples needing skilled or custodial care in the United States is 50 percent (based on *The 2014 Sourcebook for Long-Term Care Insurance*). You're way better off purchasing a plan when you're younger, but that does not mean you can't afford or qualify at older ages.

Also, *The 2008 Sourcebook for Long-Term Care Insurance* shows that 76 percent of Americans buy between the ages of forty-five and sixty-four. This protection cannot only help save you from financial ruin but can also protect your family from the heartache and burden of taking care of a loved one. Next area of similarity is Tom's touting of a laddered income annuity plan. What he is saying here is how important it is to structure your annuities to pay an income over multiple years, i.e., take one payment from an annuity now, take a second payment from another one later, and so on. This structured plan will help the cost of inflation. Over the years, you can see how consumer goods and inflation has affected retirees.

One of my beliefs in a successful retirement is to consider a second career—not necessarily at McDonald's but to consider doing consulting and/or volunteer work. This will keep you young, healthy, and happy and will keep your mind sharp.

I have always been a large proponent of having an updated will and/or a revocable living trust. This is another way of protecting your estate from probate and contestability. Your wishes will be granted after your passing. These plans offer power of attorney (someone to act on your behalf) for healthcare and financial matters. They give directives on how your estate and assets should be distributed, to whom and when. This is just another phase of having a fulfilling retirement, that peace of mind. Oh, by the way, I was late for my dinner engagement in Atlanta! I didn't realize it was a one-hour TV show on PBS. Thanks, Tom!

For many Americans, the thought of retirement is daunting. The term I grew up with was *golden years*. The days of the golden years have seemed to vanish like the gold rush. It's not too late. Many in our industry like to explain the retirement process as the "go years." Tom and I are no different. You have basically three phases of retirement.

The first phase is the "Go-Go Years." This usually consists of the first ten years of retirement. In the beginning, you want to travel, join a golf or health club, buy a boat, and be very active.

The second phase is the "Slow-Go Years." This is the next ten years of retirement. You have this boat and an old set of golf clubs, but you just don't have the energy or physical strength to be as active as you used to be. You're slowing down.

The third phase is the "No-Go Years." In this next ten-year segment, you can't go boating, golfing, or traveling because you can't. You're either unable physically or mentally.

All three of these phases have to be properly planned to meet your retirement objectives. If there is a shortcoming in just one of these phases, there could be a financial hit that could be unrecoverable. Proper planning is essential.

My promise and commitment to all our clients and future clients is to give you the best and most comprehensible information that our industry offers. This will be obtained through continuing education classes, updated licensing, financial needs analysis, annual reviews, service, business seminars and conventions, reading, and listening to specialists in the field of retirement planning. We have a team of attorneys and certified public accountants that will also assist in this process. The team concept has worked for hundreds of our satisfied clients because I cannot do all of the work, nor am I licensed to.

We work with a multitude of high-quality companies and work with a diverse clientele featuring all levels of income and socioeconomic backgrounds, from mom and pop small businesses, doctors and high-level executives, to your next-door neighbor. We do not have a minimum dollar amount to consider when working with you. We feel that limiting ourselves to clients that have "$500,000 or more" to invest is not doing a service to the general public, which so desperately needs our help and don't have those types of assets. So our company does not and will not have minimums.

With uncertainty comes risk! Our company is designed to stop those uncertainties, to stop the unexpected roadblocks like bank closures, ISIS, September 11, Al Qaeda, North Korea, Russia, and the list goes on. We are a company that will focus on safe money management strategies, guarantees, lifetime income benefits, insurance, and protection through our "sleep assurance" program.

Throughout my career, I've given numerous speeches, been quoted globally on our "sleep assurance" and have written about the peace of mind that comes with guaranteed lifetime income benefit riders. But the time is now for you to make your own call to action. Call your local experienced retirement advisor or check us out at www.foxfinancialgroup.net to get multiple opinions and design your own fulfilled, successful retirement plan.

As you can see, the modern "annua" is not what it used to be. I LOVE Annuities . . . and You Should Too!!!

NOTES PAGE

NOTES PAGE

CLIENT TESTIMONIALS

Here is just a sample of what Jim's grateful clients have to say:

"I have been doing business with Jim for over twenty years. I have found him to be sincere in his desire to help us make the best choices. He has excellent knowledge of the products available to us. He is easy to talk to and very well organized. I will continue to recommend Jim to my friends and relatives for their financial planning."

Diane M. Walsh
Purchasing Manager (Retired)
Plochman, Incorporated

"I contacted Fox Financial Group because I was concerned with my retirement income. Not having a pension, I wanted to be sure my savings would provide a secure income after retirement. Jim showed me several annuities which guaranteed a lifetime income, and provided an upfront bonus when I made my initial deposit. I am now enjoying retirement."

Terry L. Smith
Senior Vice President, Escrow Administration (Retired)
Chase Mortgage

"My wife, Beverly, and I could not be more pleased with the insurance and investment work Jim did for us. He is incredibly knowledgeable, he is personable, and most importantly to us, he is willing to take all the time needed for us to understand *exactly* what we are purchasing and why. Jim is patient and honest."

Larry Pauly
Director, Office of Admission, Chicago Region
Millikin University

CLIENT TESTIMONIALS

"I have been Jim's client since 2003. He explains things in a language that I understand, and makes me excited about my financial outlook. Jim keeps my resources in mind and offers services which fall within my needs. I am confident in my future financial stability knowing that he is there to provide his expertise and services."

Jennifer Kolbe
Senior Investigator
United States Investigation Services

"For many years, I have witnessed the sound investment and estate planning advice and exceptional service Jim extends to clients. Clients take great comfort in Jim's understanding of their specific planning needs and ultimately helping them achieve their goals."

John W. Perozzi, JD
Attorney-at-Law
Law Offices of John W. Perozzi

"I appreciated how he helped me decide what would be the best options for me as I retired. He explained everything in detail so that I could understand. Thank you, Jim, for not only being a professional but also for caring for me as a person, not a client."

Eileen Burns
Inside Sales Representative (Retired)
Mitsubishi Corporation

CLIENT TESTIMONIALS

"Jim has been a great help in handling my investment and insurance needs, as well as advising me in my estate planning. His concern and his integrity are genuine. It's a pleasure to do business with him."

Elizabeth A. Nemanich
Teacher
Hinsdale Township High School District 86

"Jim is fantastic. He spent a ton of time up front understanding our goals and current plans. He then put together a plan very specific to what we needed—not just what he wanted to sell. I've always avoided getting professional financial advice because I didn't want a cookie-cutter approach. I feel like Jim really listens."

Chris McKillip
Senior Manager
Carlisle & Gallagher Consulting Group

"Jim Fox has been doing business with me and my family for over twenty years, and we have established a loyal, respectful, honest, and trustworthy relationship. He's always there when you need him! He's a super great guy to do business with. I can always turn to him for help! Thanks, Jim!"

Susan M. Graczyk
Accounts Payable Administrator
Delta Tech Mold, Incorporated

CLIENT TESTIMONIALS

"After I was laid off, I invested my retirement in mutual funds; however, when the stock market crashed, my plans to receive a monthly dividend faded, and my initial principal investment began to shrink. A friend suggested that I contact Jim Fox to determine if he could help me. Jim is very personable, and he understands what the client wants to achieve, and he is truly interested in enabling them to realize their financial goals."

Ken Rusthoven
Assistant Vice President (Retired)
Mid-America Bank

"As retirees, planning for our future in a safe manner was imperative. Jim Fox devoted a great deal of time developing and understanding our needs. Jim is a very knowledgeable and thorough investment and estate planning advisor in whom we have placed our trust. He never pushes, he educates."

John C. Nielsen
Engineer (Retired)
Illinois Tool Works, Incorporated

"In my business, my clients are my most valuable asset. The fact that I am willing to refer my clients to Jim says a lot about the confidence I have in him."

Richard J. Fox, CPA
Certified Public Accountant and Consultant
Richard J. Fox and Associates, Ltd. (no relation)

CLIENT TESTIMONIALS

"James Fox has been my financial advisor for over ten years. In all that time, he has been an honest and reliable financial advisor. I trust him and would recommend him to anyone. It's been a profitable relationship."

Raymond D. Michelin
Market Manager
Kramer Foods

"I have known Jim for thirty years on both a personal and business level. He is trustworthy, dependable, and knowledgeable. You will benefit with Jim being on your side in today's financial market."

Michael J. Szala
President-CEO
Olympus Mortgage, Incorporated

"I didn't have much knowledge about retirement, but after meeting with Jim Fox, he answered all my questions with professional expertise and has taken care of my financial plan. Now I don't have to worry."

Patrick J. Altman
Lieutenant
Chicago Fire Department

CLIENT TESTIMONIALS

"For many years now, and continuing to do so, we have received caring, professional, and prompt advice and services from Jim that best suit our present and future needs."

Syed A. Haider
Restaurant General Manager

"Jim Fox is an excellent financial advisor. He is reliable, knowledgeable, honest, and easy to work with. We highly recommend him for your financial needs."

Ken and Gretchen Countryman
Owners of Hallmark Card store

"I have known Jim Fox for over fifteen years, when he first helped me with my BlueCross, Blue Shield, and Long-Term Care insurance policies before I retired. His service exceeds by far the normal."

George B. Hoekstra
President (Retired)
Speelman Refuse Company

CLIENT TESTIMONIALS

"Upon invitation, Mr. Fox himself visited my home and provided financial alternatives for better use of my available funds. Then he followed up to make sure I had a clear understanding and had no further questions. Any questions I had, he provided answers either immediately or with verifiable resources . . . which I did check. When I signed the contract, he took the time to explain the entire document and answer questions. He followed my purchase as closely and professionally as any I have ever known. The products offered were top rated. So goes for the man and his favorite staff member, Sharon. People of integrity."

Howard Berney

"After working with Jim for the past five years, not only has he become a good friend, he has become one of my most trusted advisors. Jim's personality, knowledge, and professionalism are a breath of fresh air in the financial services industry. I wholeheartedly recommend Fox Financial."

Chris Seats
President
Vertical Vision Financial Marketing

"Mr. Fox is very thorough and knowledgeable. We feel very fortunate to have an advisor who is creating a portfolio that will be to our greatest benefit. We will not hesitate to recommend him to others look for sound financial assistance."

Rick Howard
Senior Manager
Illinois Tollway Authority

CLIENT TESTIMONIALS

"Jim sat down with me and really understood what my financial and insurance needs were. He educated and taught me on the options I had, and I went with his recommendations. He is in the 'teaching business' and provides information that really helps you make the proper decision. His greatest service is he listens to your concerns. He gives you options, and then you decide, he is not pushing products. He gives you what you need and not what you don't. As a salesman myself, I am delightfully pleased how he has gone the extra mile. Just sit down with Jim, and you will see he is working in your best interest."

Joe Niego
Owner
Niego Real Estate

"I've worked with Jim for several years now. The best way to describe him is he is very personable and high quality. He listens to your concerns, ideas and does not push you. He's pleasant to work with and follows through with what he says. Nowadays, that is really rare. He returns calls promptly and is always on time. He has not only helped me and my family but also my mother as well. I liked the way he handled her, and that is what helped us decide to work with him. I suggest you make an appointment with Jim . . . You will not be disappointed."

Nora Barler

"Jim is a wonderful fella to do business with. I have worked with him for many years. He has helped us with our insurance, investments, and estate planning, and we used his attorney as well. I couldn't have asked for or trusted anyone more than him. He returns my call ASAP, which is what I like. If someone were to ask me for a recommendation, I would say I trust him 100 percent."

Richard Campagna
Chicago Board of Education (Retired)

"Honest, outgoing, forward, and he gives you this feeling that you have known him your whole life. He is nice to work with, doesn't come on strong, and explains everything in detail in your words, so you know what you are doing. Get your 'feet wet' with him, you will probably learn a lot. You can't go wrong with Jim."

Barbara Berry